NEW YORK REVIEW BOOKS

POETS

STEPHEN RODEFER (1940–2015) was born in Bellaire, Ohio, and studied at Amherst College, SUNY Buffalo, and San Francisco State University. As a young man, he studied with Charles Olson and got to know Robert Creeley, Allen Ginsberg, and Gregory Corso. He was one of the original Language poets. The author of many books of poems (including *One or Two Love Poems from the White World*, *Passing Duration*, and *Four Lectures*), an accomplished translator, and a prolific painter, he taught at Cambridge University, UC Berkeley, UC San Diego, and the American University of Paris—the city in which he lived until his death. More information about his life and work can be found at www.stephenrodefer.com.

GEOFFREY YOUNG was born in Los Angeles in 1944. Among his recent books of poetry are *Look Who's Talking* (2024), *Monk's Mood* (2023), *DATES* (2022), and *Pivot* (2021). His small press, The Figures (1975–2005), founded in Berkeley, California, published more than 135 books of poetry, art writing, and fiction, including Stephen Rodefer's *Four Lectures*. He has long lived in Great Barrington, Massachusetts.

Stephen Rodefer

Four Lectures

INTRODUCTION BY GEOFFREY YOUNG

NYRB/POETS

nyrb NEW YORK REVIEW BOOKS *New York*

THIS IS A NEW YORK REVIEW BOOK
PUBLISHED BY THE NEW YORK REVIEW OF BOOKS
207 East 32nd Street, New York, NY 10016
www.nyrb.com

for Jean Day, Justin Couchot, and everybody else.—S.R.

Originally published by The Figures in 1982.

Inner-cover paintings by Stephen Rodefer.
Frontispiece photograph by Bill Washburn.

Library of Congress Cataloging-in-Publication Data
Names: Rodefer, Stephen, author. | Young, Geoffrey, 1944– writer of introduction.
Title: Four lectures / Stephen Rodefer; introduction by Geoffrey Young.
Description: New York City: New York Review Books, 2025. | Series: New York Review
  Books Poets | Includes index. |
Identifiers: LCCN 2024048662 (print) | LCCN 2024048663 (ebook) | ISBN 9781681379326
  (paperback) | ISBN 9781681379333 (ebook)
Subjects: LCGFT: Poetry.
Classification: LCC PS3568.O3453 F68 2025 (print) | LCC PS3568.O3453 (ebook)
LC record available at https://lccn.loc.gov/2024048662
LC ebook record available at https://lccn.loc.gov/2024048663

ISBN 978-168-137-932-6
Available as an electronic book; ISBN 978-168-137-933-3

Cover and book design by Emily Singer

The authorized representative in the EU for product safety and compliance is eucomply OÜ,
Pärnu mnt 139b-14, 11317 Tallinn, Estonia, hello@eucompliancepartner.com, +33 757690241.

Printed in the United States of America on acid-free paper.
10 9 8 7 6 5 4 3 2 1

Contents

PASSING THROUGH New Mexico in 1967, I was taken one afternoon to Albuquerque's Okie Joe's by an old family friend, Gus Blaisdell. Okie Joe's was on the corner of University and East Central Avenue, a windowless watering hole a few short blocks from the University of New Mexico.

At the bar that afternoon were a few regulars, seated around a table. One of them was Stephen Rodefer. Then twenty-seven years old—handsome, comradely, a married father of two sons—he was teaching in the English department at the college. I didn't see him again until Laura Chester and I moved to Albuquerque in September 1969, and by this time Stephen was running the poetry reading series at the university. In 1968 he'd gotten Lenore Kandel to give a great reading from *The Love Book*. That book, legally hassled and oft-confiscated, had made of Kandel a sensation for her candid dealing with sex. And in 1970, Stephen got Charles Bukowski to fly over from Los Angeles to read on campus at the Kiva. Bukowski was just then emerging as a small-press sensation. Known as well for signing his columns for an underground newspaper "Dirty Old Man," Bukowski was new to reading his poetry in public.

By the next year, Stephen had been fired for altering the photo of a naked John and Yoko by collaging the UNM president Ferrel Heady's mug in place of Lennon's. Clearly, Rodefer wanted out of the predictable academic life he'd established. Married right out of college, and becoming a father early, now he was having an affair with the poet Summer Brenner. Soon the lovers were traveling through Mexico, and six months later they were moving to the Bay Area. The attraction of the Bay Area's lively poetry scene won out over Stephen's desire to remain a family man, though the choice was not an easy one to make. Plus, Summer was pregnant.

After the fame of Allen Ginsberg, Gregory Corso, and Jack Kerouac in the beat '50s and '60s, a new generation was just emerging in San Francisco and Berkeley. In this budding scene where readings flourished and poets danced at book parties, the romance of being young and ambitious was just the place for Rodefer. Everyone scuffled for the few jobs, but it was still possible for aspiring poets to cobble together precarious lives. Antiwar sentiment and poetry remained central to the conversations as the beer flowed, friends were made, and the social life of a generation of writers advanced.

When the National Endowment for the Arts funded the West Coast Print Center, which opened in Berkeley in 1975, many of us got jobs there, learning to make books. As small presses proliferated, the scene picked up steam. For a short spell, even Stephen worked there. His own press, the Pick Pocket Series, published his *One or Two Love Poems from the White World* and *Villon* (under the pseudonym Jean Calais), at the time. The latter, his version of François Villon's fifteenth-century French, was a brilliant breakthrough. Then around 1977 Rodefer bought a dilapidated house on Raymond Street, and it was in this house, over the next several years, that the long poems that make up *Four Lectures* were written.

An important influence on the writing of that book was the publication of Ron Silliman's *Ketjak* in 1978. A poet and theorist, Ron foregrounded the non-narrative juxtaposition of phrases and sentences (the chaste hit of direct perception might be followed by irreverent misprision, for example). The sheer accumulation of Silliman's atomized particulars keeps the reader's attention glued to the moment. With no logic but sequence, a narrative-free attention takes center stage. Ron's eclectic grabs and lean sound were the twin engines of a new poetics. That poetics is in full regalia in *Four Lectures*, which appeared complete in 1982.

Formally elegant, the book is notable for providing a substantial authorial preface—an ars poetica among other jabs and insights—and a one-page Pretext before the poems begin, and a one-page Codex after the four poems end. The Pretext and Codex are both made up of two fifteen-line stanzas, the same ample stanza Rodefer uses in the long poems. Not sonnets, nor are they meant to be, still, his fifteen-line stanzas resemble sonnets in length. Chockablock with sentences culled from all manner of sources, including radio voices, overheard street talk, previously published books, and the nutty soundtrack of his own buzzing brain waves, Rodefer's stanzas luxuriate in their own ample flesh and blood. In these big blocks of writing he can tell it like it is, and like it isn't. For example, he confronts expectation and tradition with

> Instead of what has always been known to be depth, complexity, and pressure
> of spiritual thought, you can always make it on hijinks, gloze, and chicanery,
> like a COKE machine. Do you not think?

Punkish one minute, he is studiously rebellious the next. Irony entertains, puns proliferate, and wit calls into question nearly every assumption of what poetry is, and does. Impatient with pieties, he offers advice and laughs at nonsense. To surcharge the surface, he uses bits and pieces of art and culture as educated color. In no time the reader is awash in the presence of an attractive, glancing sensibility. And somehow—by sheer tonal sophistication?—Rodefer manages to keep his genial invitation to the reader going nonstop. It is a testament to his ear for including the right goof, the tough aperçu, the absurd exaggeration. Within the capacious sprawl of long poems, there is nothing he won't include if it works a little magic in the moment. It's not that he's walking a tightrope. Still, the range of his materials and the clarity of his intellect perform an amazing balancing act. Because everything happens fast, politically sensitive lines might be preceded or followed by street jive or a hopeless truism. A social ill will find itself next to admonitions about contraception. He can be as personal as a confessional poet then as sociological as a journalist. The reader feels surrounded by elements of the real. His resistance to poetic norms is at the service of an obsessive grasp of language. And the music, even when purposely obscure or silly, is no less suggestive. To read *Four Lectures* is to ride the wild surf, wherever it leads, for the freedom and surprise of the poet's touch.

Those years in Berkeley were busy, and healthy. Nearing forty and then turning forty, he had his sons living with him some of the time. Amid various jobs there was college teaching as well as a considerable social life centered around books and readings. Just then getting active in the Poets Theater, both as an actor and a writer, Stephen said that when he would jog a few miles of an afternoon, slowly through neighborhoods, useful ideas would come to him about voice and the long line. His best role in one of the plays was as Liguras, the sadistic hotel manager in Alan Bernheimer's *Particle Arms*, in 1982.

At home, with typewriter on kitchen table and FM radio loud enough to hear, the long poems would grow as he added funny bits and carefully shaped flashes. An endless rewriter, Stephen revisited the poems time and again, changing what needed changing with each new hearing. One feature of the poems is his decision to capitalize a particular word in each stanza. I never heard him say why he chose any particular word, but nearly every stanza has one. For a brief moment, the reader's eye is hit with a typographic bump. These capitalized words invite speculation as they float by, carried along on the tide of the poem's momentum.

His public readings were mini-performances as well. Using an overhead projector, like a high-school science teacher, he would present pages on a screen for all to see, while reading them. From *Four Lectures* (for the most part), these pages were never spotless. The viewer could see edits, emendations, excisions, and scribbles. Rodefer liked showing the poem as a work in progress, even as he sounded it. Clearly it wasn't perfection he was after but actuality. The audience got a visual sense of what they were hearing, and the combo worked. His readings were never less than entertaining and educational. And they could be sensational.

Many an afternoon we'd drive with our sons to little Lake Anza in the Berkeley hills for a swim, or park at a playing field and throw a football around. It was not unlike working together on books—the camaraderie and ease—which began for the first time in 1978 with *The Bell Clerk's Tears Keep Flowing*, the title of which was a purposeful mishearing of a line in a song by Elvis Presley. The influence of Frank O'Hara on these poems is but one of that book's pleasures.

By the time we got to *Four Lectures*, in 1982, most of it had already been published in magazines. And one of the poems, "Plane Debris," had appeared as a Tuumba chapbook, printed by Lyn Hejinian. Except for the preface, the book was complete. And speaking of the preface, there is no more careful work by Rodefer than what he put into those few pages. A position paper, an ars poetica, and a challenge, the preface sets the stage for the poems like no other book I'm aware of.

Stephen had a swatch of abstract design from the Russian constructivist Liubov Popova for the cover. And we added the four factory shots of a sleek automobile being assembled, one for each poem. We'd stumbled on these photos by accident at a friend's house when we were pawing through books. We had to use them. They were positioned in the book to remind the reader that these poems were factory built as well. Not in some state-of-the-art European automotive scene but on Raymond Street, at the Rodefer manse.

Four Lectures emerged from within the period's hotbed of new writing. Reading these poems again, forty years after the book first appeared, I am reminded how much humor they generate, and how packed with insight they are. Stephen's got attitude, and the smarts to back it up. Meaning, in his hands, is nothing but action on the playing field of the new sentence. Rodefer lays it down time and again, with stamina, craft, and chutzpah. Everything is up for grabs. It's the reader's job to pick it up. And fortunately, it's a pleasure every time.

—Geoffrey Young
September 24, 2024

Writing and painting are deeply identical.
—Paul Klee

MY PROGRAM IS SIMPLE: to surrender to the city and survive its inundation. To read it and in reading, order it to read itself. Not a doctrine, but a public notice.

The city, which even before Baudelaire had been a ready-made collage or cutup of history, constantly remaking itself—a work of art, founded on an ant-hill. And every art grows out of the same collective desire which informs and compels the idea and reality of a city (Latin *colligere*, to tie together.) A district, or a ghetto, is a segmentation, an alternative version which both resists and embodies in a different fashion, that is with an opposing ideology, the original model. Hence, dialect and civil strife are alternating codes of the same phenomenon: the city does not hold together. Language, which also binds together and extends, including as it isolates, is a city also.

In such a metropolitan of history, in which the city is literally the mother, the greatest art is painting, if only by the sheer weight of the temporal. Without a city and its structures there would be no painting. The only thing precedent to painting is caves—the Gilgamesh is not as old as Lascaux.

The Greeks had painted sculpture and from the start all cultures have painted their deities. Today we have painted cities, painted conveyances, painted apartments, painted roads, painted people, even painted food. Is it not time for painted poetry as well?

A poetry painted with every jarring color and juxtaposition, every simultaneous order and disorder, every deliberate working, every movement toward one thing deformed into another. Painted with every erosion and scraping away, every blurring, every showing through, every wiping out and every replacement, with every dismemberment of the figure and assault on creation, every menace and response, every transformation of the color and reforming of the parts, necessary to express the world.

Even the words and way of language itself will suffer the consequent deformity and reformation. The color beneath, which has been covered over, will begin to show through later, when what overcame it is questioned and scraped on, if not *away.*

Political revolution answers the same process. Shapes and lines converging and diverging will formulate new ideas, the true statement of which is not fully disclosed, but fully embodied. There is a continuing direction felt within, but ordered from without. When the oppressed whole is dismantled, the parts will find a new place, more proper to them, or else all fails. In the future it will be said of such a mode, regarding its material and its language, to adapt a phrase Augustus used of Rome, that it found it brick but it left it aggregate. Deliberate decomposition is required in a state of advanced decay.

Marble is no longer the style of course. Our era promises to make the late Roman look small time, if not benign. In a world in which there are more photographs than there are bricks, can there be more pictures than there are places? I'm told that soon there will be more people living than have ever died. In innumerable ways we exist in an incomprehensible age. It is entirely unnecessary for this argument (though ultimate) to mention nuclear weapons. The signs are otherwise quite enough.

In art, just as in life, significance tends to emerge tentatively, as figures in an abstraction, or a seascape in Kandinsky, even as the figurative element reveals new structural relations which then re-define the abstraction. For example, say, Rosso Fiorentino, *Nosferatu*, or the latest improvised quartet.

Such a poetry as is suggested here is not a new concept, any more than poetry as music is. In our world it's been around at least since Blake, and was revived by Klee, Huidobro, and Picabia. My decision to take up the art again is simply carrying on, which is of course the meaning of tradition. Painted poetry is probably as ancient as the absence of machines, and with good fortune will survive the ends brought on by them.

The old form/content play has always been self-contained, like Hamlet or any good Polish sausage, somewhere between metaphor and metonymy, as the linguists would remind us, or Gertrude and Laertes. The modern world began with the first contiguity disorder, i.e. at birth, when things become wrenched from their similarity. But bent out of shape is also bent *into* shape. New replacements are expected, and they always come. We start to be fed things forcibly. We can throw up, not eat, or fold the spoon in half. Several wars are going on at once, but there is also one big war. The peace that is won with difficulty at times out of this condition will necessarily always be partial; the map will ever be fragmented and changing. The same territory with a different name makes no more sense than a different state with the same name, though we are asked in the so-called post-modern world to swallow this kind of malfeasant pitch all the time. The word itself sounds the end.

The events and systems that embody this swarming *state* of affairs have become so mixed, complex, and unconscious at once, that what is required to read it is the ultimate painting. It can be made in any number of ways, but there is no way now that it can be anything but apocalyptic. A vision is intended, rather than an explosion.

For writing is a graphic art, and a word projects either stroke or color. As it is born, a poem is drawn. It can begin with a figure or a line. It can begin to clothe a cartoon or *about* the idea of anything. It begins to paint itself. It can be made with a pencil or with a knife, with a pen or a recorder, or with a keyboard contraption that strikes the paper. It requires patience, approach, observation, technique, impulse, intent, alternation, energy, and obsession. It can be attacked by history, as well as attack history. It can be unknown and done only for itself and nothing other. Its meaning can change in time, and *always* does.

Completed, the art object is nothing but the fantasy of a given artist at a particular time. If fully worked and read totally, it will reveal all there is to know about the life of the artist, the conditions in which it was made, as well as implicate the development of art up to its example. It is shape of mind, as such. The formation of the work will literally imply the history of the species (*imply*: to fold in, envelop, embrace). Hence it will take its place at the latest point of a tradition that it will then be *carrying on*, no matter what.

Tradition as *borne*: not only what speaks to us across time, but that which we *drag along*, what we lift into the picture as well as what by a differential operation we "unload." Footstep, tread, trace, track, path, thoroughfare, method, practice, market, peripatetic *trade*, TRADITION.

I consider the enterprise of poetry therefore to be musical and graphic at once, more than literary. For how much more illuminating and amusing it is (MUSIC/MOSAIC, belonging to the muses) to compose language, or to paint poetry, than simply to write it.

As should a book be as deep as a museum and as wide as the world.

Pretext

Then I stand up on my hassock and say sing that.
It is not the business of POETRY to be anything.
When one day at last they come to storm your deluxe cubicle,
Only your pumice stone will remain. The left trapezius for now
Is a little out of joint. Little did they know you came with it.
When nature has entirely disappeared, we will find ourselves in Stuttgart.
Till then we're on the way. The only way not to leave is to go.
The gods and scientists heap their shit on Buffalo and we're out there,
Scavenging plastic trees. When nature has entirely disappeared,
We'll find ourselves in the steam garden. Evening's metonym for another
Beady-eyed engineer with sexual ideas, who grew up eating animals.
Do you like the twelve tones of the western scale? I prefer ninety.
I may work in a factory but I slide to the music of the spheres.
My job is quality control in the language lab, explaining what went
Wrong in Northampton after the Great Awakening. So much was history.

My father is a sphinx and my mother's a nut. I reject the glass.
But I've been shown the sheets of sentences and what he was
Really like remains more of a riddle than in the case of most humans.
So again I say rejoice, the man we're looking for
Is gone. The past will continue, the surest way to advance,
But you still have to run to keep fear in the other side.
There is a little door at the back of the mouth fond of long names
Called the juvjula. And pidgeon means business. It carries
Messages. The faces on the character parts are excellent.
In fact I'm having lunch with her next week. Felix nupsit.
Why should it be so difficult to see the end if when it comes
It should be irrefutable. Cabin life is incomplete.
But the waterbugs' mittens SHADOW the bright rocks below.
He has a resemblance in the upper face to the man who robbed you.
I am pleased to be here. To my left is Philippa, who will be signing for me.

Words In Works In Russian

In the ignorance that implies impression that KNITS *knowledge that finds the nameform that whets the wits that convey contacts that sweeten sensation that drives desire that adheres to attachment that dogs death that bitches birth that entails the* ENSUANCE *of . . .*

Words In Works In Russian

I was working in a factory. I'd seen BLOW UP and had a mini skirt,
AKA yack yack, ready for puking.
The yoghurt was really happening. Leaning against one of the pillars
with his axe in his hand, something different about the way he behave.
What *was* that little black thing you saw there in the white?
It sure was a lay that day. Propose to be a godfather and
carry it out. Send scarlet Brazilian orchids to the fired workers.
The two one-eyed bandits D and C, about as famous
as you could get with what they'd got.
Born on the eve of the Chilean coup and recouperating in the backyard,
saying "They got a bloody nail. They got a bloody body.
You want the serpents? They have a bloody house."
We'll have to keep the applause meter turned off otherwise
it'll just get too noisy. I get to sleep next to the night
light. I'm going to CUT myself, so I can go to the office.

The first taco I ever ate was in a graveyard on a date
in Eureka, California. Cut the crap and get on with the subterfuge.
Amsterdam, a good place to be stone. Pathetic Bethesda.
Strike the mojo and give your hand a rest.
My hand became my enemy in 1983. What is brilliant
becomes boring, in the future's perspective, like another
zombette with one uncertainty piled on the other.
Continue the serious action. The note to Harold Fondren.
For sure this is a boisterous barnyard. Very Reverdy.
Give me a bite so I can stop talking too.
Life is a tangle and it's LIVID, because of the chemicals.
I have no checking account, no thyme, no marjoram.
Many times I wondered when they took my daddy down.
The owners can eat pain. A caballero without a horse.
Chairman Mao will never pick up a telephone again.

Begin to think of cruelty as the inability not to be cruel and try
to stay decent. The unearthly crocuses. I wish I were
assured of my condition. Now that we are all here,
will something always continue to stand still, like an agent?
God will hold it against you if you don't believe in anti-matter.
At last, the something of prose. Cello V. My back.
Who is the figure the TEXT of which we are now the event?
You're wrong, master, just and wrong.
Little Joe's. A mural, an aria, the beach. Better than a therapist.
Inscrutable, colossal, and alone, the sands stretch far away enough.
Pretty flashy lighthouse you got here. Cercamon, Marcabru,
and Blackburn too. This certainly is a beautiful "spot."
Entre la campagne, et la ville. I'll call you.
Endymion was obscure too. There follows a wrangle.
See you at La Mamelle or The Stud. Tipica Cienfuegos. Odetta Mo.

Longevity is out of the question. Play by bending.
Van Gogh's pear trees shining like shark paint in the skull-like flowers.
People in bed with themselves do not really sleep with each other,
they're just Buddhists in love. You dream you are the master
of Nottingham and all of a sudden, creditors.
School children are a joy to be held. Peeing in the garden
behind the Preandergestraat, I apologize to the universe
for being alive so long. I was drawing a tree at a RODEO,
and they were throwing down a lot of cowboy boots from the balcony.
Fantastic variations on a nightly theme.
Matthew Smith's nudes. John Martin's apocalypse.
The fairy fellow's master stroke. The Cholmondeley Sisters.
Words in works in Russia. Out the window may be
out to lunch for those who fuck only once, but what about us monks?
Judgment is thistledown. Poetics is job application. Economy was dead in the water.

Dutch has dykes that make the germen palatable with their tongues.
Then there's Bunny at Tassajara. Apply nivea cream and be dumb.
In regards death everybody is a mystic.
Cheeseburgers may be required in Paradise.
House playing geraniums pretending to like tables, windows.
Pure imitation and learning look up to Maxwell Bodenheim in their mistake.
Ted has a knack of using YOU without using you and *that's* a snack.
It's blood that makes us love, at the Galerie Fiolet.
For dinner is a cheap side of poultry; sleep is for the restless.
Buy film! for the emotions to take place at the crack of dawn.
We must give up our tradition and write like ghosts released to their machines.
Whereas in the Blue Room at home Roosevelt invented polio,
picking apart daddylonglegs. Somewhere you'll find an apartment
which is without a Belgian toilet. All the cats of Venice
were brought from Egypt in order to consume the canal mice.

Beautiful Sonia Delaunay. Kerb your tyres. Brooklyn Yoghurt
Chewing Gum—*la gomma del ponto*. Otto Dix, *Portrait
de la journalist*, beside the great Malevitch.
Just in case they had of, I merely thought I wouldn't.
Bill Berkson in an extraordinary pair of wicker sunglasses,
smoking a Kent. Whatever wears you out, you wear out.
Just call the press HARP SEAL, Richard, and forget it.
The nail is unison. I just want to be social and suck, writing
the treatise on suicide *Not To Be*, an incidental Spicerian stanza.
This time *your* water is golden and *I* smell like a bad wing,
recalling the witchcraft of Kathleen. I have played
the horses *Crucible, Nom de Plume, Ecstasy,* and *Werther*,
bleary eyed at the scene of last night's debauchery and drinking
with the dunce's advantage. The moon is for the eye and it is a sin to step on it.
Don't believe except what you imagine. Visit all graves with masses of newly devised beauty.

We must go our own way but remember we are going to have to take *them*
with us. The specter brother who got the pistol but not the STAMINA.
The only problem is choosing which bedroom to get, because there are so many.
Grace Hartigan's post doctoral work leaves one cold, for instance,
while Marsden Hartley is terrific. So much for time and development.
When the student sits down, the teacher appears.
I hold a little Hoolihan in mind. If you will not go with
to see Wendy on her stilts, then you are a piglet.
I have my cadets and I wish they had less power over me this year.
We who find ourselves in these bodies maturing anyway.
I rilke don't trust it. I'd rather have dog shit on my lawn than bottled water.
Instead of what has always been known to be depth, complexity, and pressure
of spiritual thought, you can always make it on hijinks, gloze, and chicanery,
like a COKE machine. Do you not think?
The depression that comes from not being granted is not very impressive.

Most of the fish I have known if they had *had* bicycles wouldn't have been eaten.
By the day what is the record for bank robberies in New York?
Can you believe some English actually made his homage to the BEACH
BOYS by cutting an electronic collage of their seminal work?
No, of course you can't. But a California girl *is* a potential song.
Music becomes gilt. Glom onto some redolent creep and pretend
that you are in love. I'm sick of daylight. I want God.
My name is Gaston and I would like you to make it out to cash.
I don't care an iota to be an atom in the dynamic of ordinary interface.
Remember Toscanini, after all, conducting *La Bohème* in Turin in 1896.
A sure sign of victory, seeing a lot of sable coats and crocodile bags leaving Iran.
This monastic but indulgent plateau series for dissonant and enduring blacksmiths,
moving from laughter to famine in a cycle of determination in which
art does not lament what ears have sung all to themselves.
Still, strange to grow a bush of parts, and exemplary depart.

Here go one. Silent reading! everybody, silent reading!
Meine liebestraum, meine liebesfreund, meine liebestod.
Once upon a time there were four rabbits running along
toward their mischief. This, as in "with this ring I thee wed."
Charles Olson's broad side. We've got bejillions of flowers,
for the Louis the XIVth whose identity has never been established absolutely.
And I was in it at the time when my bed was burnt to the ground.
Not a good prospect from which to become the reigning *Butterfly* of your time.
Strange still to be 28 or 32, and face imminent uterine disaster at any moment.
God may not exist, but he has certainly spoken quite a bit.
You can form a farm, register Democrat, and control more
than ten percent of the county vote, making like *The King
of Marvin Gardens*, a marred but stimulating flic.
Wasn't it Shakespeare who said, "That was not a nice letter"?
And then I started to get this feeling of NAUSEA.

Deaf is lisp for death. Pass me a little of that *petit* pain.
It's supposed to get cloudy and not be so marvellous tomorrow
(rain?). I'm holding out for some black underwear from beyond.
There are two truly effective things women can withdraw
to teach you you have not acted correctly—your children and themselves.
I'm getting out of here and it ain't gonna be on no public transport.
Some people's half lives are longer but that doesn't mean they're lead.
We just want to be a part of NATURE and stay there.
Cornelius Cardew's piano works on proletarian themes. Finadar 6011.
Well I ate breakfast now what? Ursula Oppens plays Frederic Rzewski.
Van. VSD 71248. Dying in a vacuum of endless work
won't work so don't try. Do you have any bottled sweat?
You'll make it hard to sleep alone in the Goetheneum,
even when dead. About as obvious as Dante being a druggist.
Overcome by the percussive element you start up the stairs, and they backfire.

The opportunities of this world have become so scarce
that people have stopped applying for them.
The result is that periods of deprivation
have become much longer. People who used to spend
a few weeks or a month seeking a job or a place
to live, or a lover, now are looking for years,
or not bothering to look at all because they know
it's not there, or it's too expensive, or they can't
have it because they haven't already got it.
When breakdowns occur under this kind of UPPED ANTE
(or you could say people are sitting at a table where
there are no longer any cards being dealt),
they are likely to be much more severe—
it is altogether a cruel and unusual turn of events,
but out of it we should not expect a new Constitution.

Let me say this bang out. I wonder what thoughts Hardy was absorbed in when he died.
Every day is a day for a lovely factory worker. I probably like this alot
less than you do. Some people are more like porticoes than patios.
Thereby are they kept from their proper vacation. In love remove your antlers.
Mal Waldron and Charlie Haden take care of all the passion questions.
I am one of the people in the great CHAIN of being.
Now where's the food, where's the money, and where is the love.
You know Hatha Surrender, Dean of JFK's School of Consciousness?
Women and watches have one common power. Byron got his club
foot because his mother wore a corset when she was pregnant.
Sometimes *screams* can give birth to incredible moments,
and eyes depend on you's and a yes for however many sous.
The whales beached in the Bay of California when Charlie Mingus passed.
When we talk of freedom let us have the memory to speak of it
in a Biblical way. Burn the Christmas green at the Pacific.

Feel the original heat of the earth's breast.
The only country with a higher percentage
of its population in prison than the USA
is South Africa. Content and form have always been the same,
only vice versa. Prince Charles owns Dartmoor. The only poetry
which really interests you is your own, but you don't bring this up
since it seems so reactionary and you know it's the same with your friends.
Thank god though that in spite of pretending to be some rock
regardless of what you think you are, you are becoming something else.
Several of your friends are happy at the NEWS too.
Not on your kodachrome. Would you? Nice matin.
Molly is Jane People. Lon Nol is worse than Pol Pot?
Lost one of your glassies? Just ordinary brain damage
due to the difficulty of asking for company.
It's a wonder all the tall trees are not lying down on strike.

In Tehran to show pleasure they throw candy and rose water
on each other in the street, knowing how.
A dry, brown mushroom from Menlo Park with no price.
On his deathbed Brueghel instructed his wife to burn some of his paintings
as they could get her into trouble, lending personality to his oeuvre.
Paranoia is a carful. Step into her bed.
A woman so preserving she wouldn't sleep with you in a bomb shelter.
So do not flush this toilet unthinkingly there is a water shortage.
Take a shit with a friend, picking up on the side Karl
Marx' comic novel *Scorpian and Felix*, the dark little SAVAGE.
Let me answer with red cheeks and white flesh all
such questions of steady income. If you ever need
a rubberband, it's in the front yard.
Marching anciently and out of sight,
the lift is cool and the countess dunked.

I have an ardor for orgy but it is not an ardor.
Debauchery dies in sedated children, counsellor.
The non-Indian support coalition for indigenous people.
Pawning his coat to buy potatoes, his mother wondered naturally
when he was going to stop writing about it and make some.
Boyfriends were dispensible in the weather in which every other day was capital.
As in Steve Benson's work *Alligators Can't Be Intimidated*.
I am a machine condemned to devour books and then throw.
Smelly recent past. Truly fertile older history.
For carbuncles try port, try arsenic, try opium.
Suffering from syphillis and losing his epiderm,
poor Schubert found solace in composing music he
hardly ever heard AIRED. Plain print, that's what
we long for a century later. Write a long work called *Now Wait a Minute*
or *The Radio Controlled Torpedo George Antheil Patented With Hedy Lamarr*.

How's your suffering zombette, now she's heavy into chicanisma?
There's that grungy cur death, making its first tentative scratch at the door.
Let's have another drink. Another penultimate libation on the grave
of the muse before bed. With HUE like that of some great painter,
who dips his pencil in the gloom of earthquake and eclipse.
Everybody's at some fault. The British Railroad wouldn't hire Marx because
his handwriting was so awful. Remember Irving Flores.
When you are dead to everything, you might as well *be* dead.
The house plants *are* starving for some birth control.
Another quality job by Colleges and Romeo.
Fuck penises! Stand backish. Figone, Provincial, and Maple.
Urine therapy. Berkeley. Journeyperson work.
Napoleon, the inventory of the concealed weapon.
A flying fish high over Twenty Languages. Ruptured Gringos.
Hard Bargain. Johnnie Squeekie. Exuma Cay.

As you expand become all evocative. Upper level
obsession. A green Egyptian by a muddy nail.
Let's just say they enter a room with dubious godsend.
Let me be a Christian to your lion and end this circus
once and for all. The noble look of deep trouble.
Tell him I send him my love and we should be together soon.
After Henry Cowell spent these years I now live
locked in prison as a homosexual, he did not want to be
differentiated from the public and his music understandably
changed direction and became more international.
Dinky Baby. Lisa AKA Chocolate. Lil' Rocky. No
egrets. No LAGOON. The reason the so-called ecology movement
appeals so much to the rich and leisure class is that the country
is the work place of the rich and leisure class. It is the fact
that their environment is being threatened for the first time

on the same level that an industrial worker or someone
in the ghetto has been accustomed to for a life time.
Enter the dope lawyer as a friend of the earth.
The Moment's Pause Hydrotherapy Gallery NEXT
to the MacDonalds in Mill Valley. Though it may not be
smart checkers, I've got my bindle packed and think I'll head on
out, before they blow the goobers off me.
Nothing is true, but everything is real. Bob says "He
sure eats alot!" What did you expect, a hunger artist?
Remember that the sun is big and your mother lives in 11-A.
Remember the triumph over poverty that reaches into jail,
and that you may never touch that creature whom you love.
Vibe means tremulous power, as in *vibrato*.
Of Tanguy I sing. Bivouac. In the guest room of the Apollo Wax Museum.
A man of color, with all of the calluses, who might as well pitch.

Sleeping With The Light On

That which is heard from the lips of those to whom we are talking in our day's affairs mingles with what we see in the streets and everywhere about us as it mingles also with our imaginations. By this chemistry is fabricated a language...which shifts and reveals its meaning as clouds shift and turn in the sky and sometimes send down rain or snow or hail...Thus to say that a man has no imagination is to say nearly that he is blind or deaf. But of old poets would translate this hidden language into a kind of REPLICA of the speech of the world with certain distinctions of rhyme and meter to show that it was not really that SPEECH. Nowadays the elements of that language are set down as heard and the imagination of the listener and of the poet are left free to mingle...

Sleeping With The Light On

I don't want to make a disclaimer beforehand but it wasn't raining in the capital.
Who's the woman with Attila? Don't all start at once but begin anyway.
More is what ensues when it is no longer the same. Half way between
here and God change place as in a novel, continuing to sing as though
it were verse. Pride doesn't speak. It kicks its foot out of the cradle
to disturb the mobile meant to hang over its slumberpoo like a waterfowl
on pilot. Out of paint make light, like a painter. Go far enough
so this *phrase* will become itself. One voice can't date address any longer.
The LYDIAN MODE. The chartreuse in the distance of the homerun.
A woman is dating an undertaker. She has a right. He wants her to lie down
beside the still. Birds are in the trees and they know it. They don't
drink. They consider the beauty of hills when they are on them and when
they are not. Something in nature that is definitely not coffee.
Comes a tide to make the clams open up, into the figment called dusk.
Jealous teachers poison their pupils; gooselivers, the favorite food of Mozart.

Some feisty old school teacher assigned the boy to write something
about his love of rocks. He bought the rocks and the rocks won.
The trilobites piled into their cars. Others run until their toes leave
their bodies. Left books under bush in lot across from school,
would you mind getting them for me before it rains? signed Eremite the First.
Everything is permanent *and* passing, over and above the undergrowth.
Who's next to be beheaded cannot decapitate another.
Life without Yum Yum is unbearable. When a married man loses
his head, his mate is buried alive. This vermouth needs more angelica root.
The automobile has become the natural predator of night animals.
The refrigerator starts to fucking hum. The singing East Bay and beyond.
I saved you from enlightenment and you saved me from lesbianism.
When I say me it's a figure of speech. Just another poet AGOG for foam.
Look at all those f-stops up there. Eventually everything becomes all stars.
Are you who they call Poochie? *Chi*huahua! We . . . . . are . . . . . dead . . . . . men.

Build a closet and get a grip on life, and don't forget to kiss goodnight.
The only thing like the ocean is early morning light. Take a big, sulking bruiser
like yourself, and teach him to make love. The boys we mean are not inclined.
Find yourself an affinity group or better yet an assault group and dig the query.
If poems could kill, alot of people would die.
On March 22 don't miss the POET'S DINNER at prestigious Spenger's,
not forgetting to scratch your forehead where it accomplishes its merger
with your temple and you'll think of more. Going to Granny's.
Nothing changes but the weather. Immediately arresting are all gorgeous
slow movements. Coming around the mountain accompanied by infibulation,
the lips are trembling but the eyes are mad. In this country one must be
quick to rim and slick to laugh, despite the multi-nationals.
At least in Korea they have their head man do it at a dinner party.
Cut these sentences and they have little Caesars. Not inclined. NOME by any
other name would be very different. And so it is with me—filament and sabotage.

The text this morning don't hallelujah but it's ready
to commit treason without fail. I have a radio phonograph and plan to have more.
The smart money hits the canvas as the yokel says his piece.
Good news for pregnant smokers. Like as not you gotta AIR your QUIPS.
They laugh but they moans too and what is it to you to do, strangely satisfying?
There should be nothing but a continual prologue to liberty.
Theorize that you're listening and it's a state,
instead of taking the job wrapping or calling for the casino.
The night is pricking on plain juice. Consumption and reply.
Getting off in a vicarious vein. Basketball drivel. Dependent tunic.
Thinking in screams. You have dript blood in the dictionary. Now get some TISSUE.
You have spilt ink on the carpet. Go poison a squirrel and rip up all your books.
For God's sake batter swing. Throw the stranger in the third row out.
Jackson didn't like to be doing stuff with coffee, he would
throw it down. Happiness was nothing more than the escape from Greek.

Pick a life and live it. I think I'll go down to the iron works
and order some chains. Shreveport and shriveltechnics. I inhabit the language
the world heaps upon me. Branch water on the rocks.
Papa's baby rows across the great Salt Lake of suicide
in her black lipstick, one stroke ahead of the DELUGE, wearing a verb.
Far from the rampant scalper's early tickets you could shut a beaver up
in a bedroom, and it would immediately start building its dam.
It may be fun but only as long as you can stand it, with a quartet of amigos.
It is crazy to get out of bed without a mission, but never has there been witness
to a burnoose berserker than yours. Our life is typical of the social conditions
under which literature occurs in spite of its no longer commanding high political
reward. Why should a dog a rat? Why should an assassin a despot? Why should Iran Iraq?
The simple, uncomplicated life is over and painfully you are born repeatedly
with layers of self-consciousness which you must simply ignore. The working poet
takes a can of V-8 juice out of his pail, and smiles at the man next to him.

It would be difficult to determine just what would be the right moment
to cease to be Hart Crane. The evacuee and the chiasma.
It was dark but they could be seen to be riding down on us hard,
night's plain pricks. Fucked in the head by the pigtail, I sense and dive
and tumble under the dogwood. I fire and strike the leg of the leader.
For shit for sure. When your face gets pasted and you can't find your way home.
While it may never be more than a matter of semantics, the negative
side of the coin gets more publicity than heads. LIMPID EMPEDOCLES
Implicit nix. We needle to amuse. Eyes spelt yes. Alps on the moon.
I'll just sit quietly in my chair and admire you, avoiding the temptation
of nympholepsy. You speak to me in SIGN language and I'm buying it.
I have cultivated this mild hysteria for fear of ecstasy.
I came by to kill you but you weren't home. Der Deutscher bist fucked.
Cremated into the handful that was you indeed. Epistemology and fatigue.
Anton von Worms certainly lives up to his name in the St. Gereon Altarpiece.

It has become necessary to don dirtiness in order to *de*scribe it.
I've never known a more insightful headache remedy. Slip out
into the city and add your ochre to its already cochineal.
Just smoke the facts, whatever your reel to reel needs and ask
how many citizens know that salt has sugar in it. Take looks
and be quotidian, and realize that history doesn't trap but releases you.
Calculate your work in terms of hunger. Excuse yourself from your duty
to advise the young, so as to continue to figure it yourself.
In having to look after the imprisoned, people tend to become criminals themselves.
Andrea Schiavone's MARRIAGE OF CUPID AND PSYCHE makes you want to get out
of analysis and make a night of it. Snap your fingers and be transformed.   .
Nothing should ever be done that does not deserve infinite repetition,
for that is what it will get. This is what history is about,
when it is not making you rich. Why be subtle and false?
The future is poison and we are caught kissing the cup.

Now or never is the time for verses. I'm ready for the gig,
but I don't know about the spot. Personally I have a distaste for
miscellany and am absolutely programmed against Personism per se.
It is the attitude of the spine to develop into an opinion, leading to your malady.
Laughter is the reverse of aspiration. Beards are good for eating women.
The sun is captivated by the dew's beauty, and longs to view it more closely.
It is best not to identify too strongly with your troubles.
There are some poets who in a snowy field should be silent.
Nothing so dry as DROPSY, but thinking makes it so.
They left Keats' name off his book so it would sell better.
Ordinarily you'd have to be a genius to do what he did, but he simply thrust
his pick in the ground and the fossils came tumbling out.
Masturbating he thought, if only I could satisfy my hunger so easily.
The father of the country was a six four man with a weak voice and slow mind,
which made it inconvenient for him to move fast, so he stayed.

I think I'll just call in tired today and not make the scene at the tryouts
for a bird in flight. The lianas are turning over their sunny whispers.
Impossible to embark on anything and not flirt with going overboard.
Cooking carrots and onions for dinner cannot satisfy sweet teeth.
Lachrymose vinaigrette. Victorious dyslexia. He laughed just because it was
not allowed. It occured to him to refuse to open tin cans for cats for instance.
Do not give up desiring what your cat has, understanding that not getting it
is a reward also, as the philosophic frame it will lend automatically
to your consciousness will be invaluable in reckoning hum and worth.
Rimbaud got his leg cut off before he died, but Verlaine had published
his posthumous verse even before that. Early piss-elegant imitations
of Wallace Stevens. At the foot of the jetty, an Argentine chair.
O claquepatin, O mantra, O pie alamode, are you who they call Poochie?
Mayakovsky mistook the EAST RIVER for the Hudson and missed meeting Lorca
in New York, the black dog trotting down the street holding an eraser in its mouth.

A woman is ironing, lending an ear to a would-be suitor.
Waking, it was noon. In reality she is in love with the jailer's assistant.
It is the destiny of the lover to be rejected, of the spouse to be indispensible.
Your mother is glad to wash your sheets, if ultimately she is no good for you.
If you are a mother you can do anything you please, and it too will be a mother.
No wonder kids sleep at mid day. They dream more, so they can be ready.
A grown man, he opened the can of Chicken Of The Sea and tucked a pinch
of TUNA in his cheek. Men don't love women, though they try.
Quotation marks are question marks when talk still counts,
as in a Forties movie. Which is the past participle of lust, lair or lore?
These musicians have such a developed sense of rest and false starts
that their music resembles nothing sometimes so much as it does a fitful sleep.
You have a new ribbon and some free time, what do you want to refer to something for?
when you could be practising the virtuoso stunt of never saying anything.
All of you who are ugly turn your radio off for a minute please.

How do you like your CUISINART? The second step in pure creation
is to become ecstatic when eternity uncovers itself. The first
is to make a place for it. My washing machine said "Guggenheim,"
because it freed me to be a writer, its dark veins bruise blue.
The passing boy looks at the Bacon on the wall and says YUCH.
I admire your body and you begin to scream. Really ridiculous to be a writer,
when your basic gift is speech. At the grave of Peter Stuyvesant,
the rookie with the printing press is reading the tape recorder.
Glamors and blue chips sharing honors and scoring their solid advance.
Don't you tuck me in without my unwilfulness! Who wrote the Ode to Delphine?
Oh him. No shoes, no shirt. Your neck is tight, but you're incredibly receptive.
I wear CUFFLINKS because I am an ecology freak. I may be perverted,
but I'm not insatiable. You mean you like women with toothpicks too?
For luxury see Pisanello. Everybody tends to look alike up close.
The sack calls me to horizon. Many more anniversaries of natal day.

Loathsome narrative. Insignificant event. Expedient idea.
A TUB is of *course* liable to cheese, but athletics is not my game.
Do you wear hats or just otherwise make use of them?
On paper at least we can believe in immortality. Bella Abzug is not ague proof.
Sooner or later you know you're going to have to sell somebody.
The artfulness that allows the living to die and the dead to live.
That ain't art, it's morphine. An indescribable feeling to boot.
Diffusion can be complex and lead to disintegration
or it can a way of life be, even a joy, staring into the lake
of all former reflection. The leaves are really rusting.
What is the closest candy to school? Shut off art static.
Passing so and so's loft, shout THROW DOWN ART MONEY!
You honor me by asking me to leave a world to which you belong.
You may not have swallowed the one about the dream,
but you swallowed the one about the magazine. Better write than read.

Give him head he'll prove a jade. Nugatory and jejune, pal.
Stag leap dry creek. Minimal derail. Donative speech.
The one to watch in the fourth is FICTIVE MUSIC.
The state of Massachusetts will have enough troops to handle the future.
A striking teacher is refusing to continue making faulty students,
or less than a street cleaner. Unable to attack become more bird
than flutist. A spoon of tahini and swig of kefir for the denatured teenager.
Once a system goes unchecked into a larger system, subsequent attempts
to check its original malady will bounce back as incredibly backward,
as indeed they will be, on the journey to American history.
Economics is a description of the point at which a society finds itself
between birth and destruction. Too much blame is laid on Arabs.
Good evening. Bankers think the recession won't be quite so bad. It is possible
for a woman to touch a man on the job mainly near the foothills, but the lobbyist
buttonholes them before they get to the REVOLVING DOOR of public service.

Are you a name artist? or just otherwise another writer whose main idea
of what to do in life is become famous. Better never to remember or to learn.
One's experience is hardly ever with one. O one hundred hours.
PERSONALITY is the persistence of others' sense of you,
taking you for something you are not, but in their minds there you are.
I am here to deal with English, not to be a mate in taxis.
Still testing your generation on the Drāno? Brian Eno simply isn't Not Vitál.
Bridget Bardot gets to utter the *pièce de résistance* of all French cinema:
J'ai peur, and it's before Godard. Now I call that DARN innersting.
Warts are wonderful structures, which can appear overnight on any part of skin,
like mushrooms on a damp lawn, full grown and splendid in the complexity
of their particular cancer. Information rafts through the air.
An at bat. SOAPY NUTS. Just another extremely kissy baby destined to be
one more hardon scraping by. If you don't jelly up the ring, heaven will know
your kind. Is this thing on? Am I coming across some Monongahela or other?

Derail this choo choo at your own risk. We are forming a new society of campanology.
House painters climb into the sky to make their bucks, what's your excuse?
In the year of the dead beats prepare to make apologies for a bad mistake.
Step over the threshold and rake what you have mown,
but don't ever agree with anyone to waste their time by asking for it.
It's ALL happening. Writing and police records were devised at once.
Rome was not built in a day, but they're working on it.
What'll it be, Harold in Italy or Maggot Brain?
Inspiration is a conspiracy. You'll be looking at the moon,
but you'll be seeing Mussolini. Though recall the opera director
is the number three man in Austria. Let's knock the other argonauts up too.
To fornicate, the artist stops working. I can just see myself,
sitting on a horse for the next century. I challenge you to a book.
Absence is just another form, an echo on schedule, a SYNECDOCHE.
So, to speak you walk out of your slippers and into my soliloquy.

Restate the whole culture. We now know what it's like
to be without a habitat. If the alternative were bombing,
there'd be no problem. Let's go out for some dumb song
later on. Isn't this behavior as telling as another?
Take a mild guess. He'll've not eaten. This is no skill, it's a scratch—
like a history, like a legend, like a Sol LeWitt. Tatum was trying
to break Stingley's neck but he didn't expect to. Fay Wray being taken
by that nice ape. It gets the fauvist rave. It's so hard
to be an eager young person, so deadly to be regretful. Doesn't it occur
to you that some day not far off both of us will no longer be living?
The plan is the body thanks alot. A human carcass is no better than a chicken.
This heroine is addictive and I know whereof I speak.
Bland white night bidet, without the need and softening of what is.
The spiritual substance that is you, body, refusing forever
the wishfulness of the visible. CALLED only because you left your feet.

He types on his machine the brain of life.
I am in a French church. It is a wedding. I must stand up.
To please my friend better I will put on this pretty hat.
Amputate the freckled bosom and make me bearded like a man.
Choleric, phlegm, and funny bone. Ordinary intercourse.
Cuisinarts galore. If you don't buy this urinal, I'll shoot this dog.
And then what? The fucking redeemer leaves. Winds right wrong.
Life is a waste of money. In the NAIROBI STEREOPHONIC DINER.
I am not a sonnet, you are not a sea urchin, and this is not a poetry contest,
comrade. No use being total while still growing. We live by chants
and cannot wait to go down. After dark our motto
is never pee in the toilet; our vow, never to forget the track
India left on the ocean floor when it moved away.
The plan is not to be noticed when playing, but to be missed when not.
We are NOT EXCITED to be a friend of Voznesensky. He kisses us anyway.

And so an inexplicable feeling of sadness overcame me at the xerox machine today.
All the people in their pants, with the LOOPS but not the hammer.
The great American artist yet to emerge will emerge too late.
Unfair attitude. Out of paint, light. Out of words, a music.
How much does your drawing weigh? Give it some color they will call by your name.
It was to be one, and so we make do with MORE. A genius tale
which missed the door and must go round again.
Davy Tough is a protector, caved in and vexed, but in a sky which lasts.
Tired of staying home, go away. In sight of land, shore leave.
The art of geese, perfectly realized in the city. The art of being
perfectly stuck with yourself. I'm prepared and accustomed,
in a room that is quiet for no one who listens.
If it weren't for you I wouldn't be here, though it *is* a beard of uncertain returns.
Singing, the hummingbird is clicking on an airy straw, percussively.
Anyway call and tell me all the little newses.

Plane Debris

Who will believe my VERSE *in time to come*
LIES *in the spine which it entombs.*

Your ACCENT *is something finer than you could purchase in so removed
a dwelling.*
I have been told so of many...I have heard many lectures.

Plane Debris

My mind to me mangles iron. An error is mirror to the truth
than any statement claiming to be true. I saw a tree and the idea
arose from memory that it was a mango tree. The past is made of brain cells.
We wouldn't have time if we didn't think about it. Thought creates matter
that nature didn't think to. How incredibly perceptive
that women have decided to paint themselves in every age. Measurement
means distance, and is political. They fight fire for instance,
but though they burn they do not fight themselves. One of the Bauhaus lovelies
on the staff of WET can do the awesome graphic. My name will be Money,
but you can call me Change. Antiphilus, Antipater,
do not let the prick think. Her Harry thinks she is too much.
I am exactly as old as you ART. Wonder in and spy the pond.
Truth is, most state of the art is actually edge of the park. Out one ear
and in the other. Hearing lists on an off day. Woods wave leaves.
The town signs. Here the papyrus begins to tatter. The rest is loss.

Still be kind and eke out the performance with your mind.
If you have to cough, cough. You think you know everything,
but you only know half of it. You must reveal your self,
your time, and the structural development of art up till now.
Let us match our racquets to their balls. Upon a filet
balance a model to propose a spread. Just the right hint of everything,
pushed through a sieve. The logic of any gross natural array.
We live in bags, presented and ready to be taxed, feeling the necessity
of blocking the choreography behind *any* massive confusion.
The imagination wells—first one tip, spin off, then sea mist,
drifting and swell, spindrift. The repetitive structures of the intellect
at attention. Spit shined rhyme. Saluted rhetoric.
By now you look ready to stick your thumb in a dyke and become a heroine.
Spread your TEETH and lift your nostrils ups, flying with your bike in your arms.
National guardsmen are throwing up all over, and so we enter the blow-torch world.

Like history, a man is a lesson. As soon as you learn it, no need for class.
This doesn't mean that you leave the world that imagines them.
Dying with the tide turning, bustle courage up.
Trade fame for sustenance and safety, to be halted in a familiar path,
guarded by babies and old women. Derivation and other particulars,
affably used. The nose as wet as a pen, cold as stone.
Still crying out for company and the sack. It is the same for us all,
so God bless you. The lesson in ENGLISH is really a lesson in French.
Let me entreat your succor. If you are dead, I'll slumber.
If there is breath, I'll mark the glass. The dull ear is dumber than night.
If the enemy is an ass, speak lower. I love the lovely bully.
We know enough if we know we are subjects. Everything waits
for you, for which I am grateful. And confusion is mineral.
Achieve me and you can sell my bones. Base weed—
my horse is my mistress and gives me a bad back, at the tip of the pouring dark.

You see how queer it is. You see one big dipper. You see them all.
On Thursday we have all the best acts from Wednesday.
Take off them schoolboy glasses. I must be surrounded
by great art, or thrive. I'll be the one in the C-cup by the door.
Break my mind to me in broken English. It contents me.
If you want to be a woman, or a man, be sure and always keep a can
of evaporated funk on hand. In little rooms the tongues
of people light. Mock me intelligently if you know
the half of it. I cannot tell what is like me. After all,
I speak your tongue and you mine. Nice customs.
Great curtsy. Besotted traveller…, if I might BUFFET for a moment,
does peace nurse arts? Put it in writing and send me a copy.
A shale, pale English shore, more sure than France. I expose
myself to language. It makes a goal. I am open mouthed.
It arrests me. The crowd roars. They long to eat English.

The sign at school said "Get Smart With Me."
The bugle by a dead corporal. The gag order. Autumn in diapers.
The dew on the asleep wino's beard. A map of the clouds for John Cage.
Up parasol! Devil de ville and hold the host.
Dimly imagine me sunny, and I appear, trailing oompapas
for your juvenescence. There is no other tourniquet.
A popinjay is better than a teaser. Type own power.
Beautiful TAWNY crystals of vouchsafe night.
An eskimo in shades. A meerschaum for this scenery.
An aborigine with a Camel. He is on to her.
He puts her on. She could care less. Translate saxophone
sex. I'm not sorry I saw that, but I am I thought about it.
Well met hiccup. A lakelet by a foothill. Dial-A-Phone. 911.
Outside chance. It was in short the servant of Venus.
She wanted to fuck him in the phaeton, but he said nothing of the kind.

His methadone had no technique, but nevertheless it did the trick.
On a stick on my grave put a life jacket, or Joe's, or some asbestos
gloves, against the storm to come. Make spirits rise. Bells on bobtail ring.
Art Pepper's ventral hernia is strapped up so he can play.
I'd kick you, if I didn't think you'd enjoy it.
Frau Crocodile happens to be the air-raid warden.
And I'm not made of SOAP. I love my wife, but I need all of her.
Iodine 129 accumulating in the thyroid. When you're dreaming lucky baby,
you wake up cold in hand. Life in this family is one
subpoena after another. The annoyance of another speed bump.
Has the chamber been laid in this week? Oral jelly.
A gondolier or a matador, I don't care which. Just make sure, laughing.
Do not dive under the boat or sail. Get up before dawn and want park.
The only place you can still hear Mass in Latin is Peking.
So listen we could use some sheets out here in the mountains.

In other scandals about Washington Mr. Bush says he is clean clean clean.
Now that James Wright is dead, I have to keep the BELLAIRE-MARTINS FERRY axis alive.
If it's not any good, I don't want to find out till later.
Don't you ever cakewalk into town, or will you be agreeable
to blanketing the globe with phones? Venom reduces quality.
Certainly. She was living proof that a woman could be both sharp and a cookie.
Hitch up the PEONIES. Felons and thugs don't fall from trees.
They make tools of them, and live there. They spit on the burghers below.
Let them eat phlegm. The grooves are in the metal mother and this is the best
way to reissue. It's logical that as property goes sky high,
cars should get closer to the ground. The FBI seizes Iran's de Koonings.
The fat Burns guard is reading FATE on the 14 Mission. The Pancho Villa
Oil Company. SKY RAINS PLANE DEBRIS. If I am to be killed by a piece
of falling wing, or drenched in jettison, I'm game. Who could skip town?
I can't move to the country or settle down. I need the material.

The only accurate way to view the people is on the bus.
Nice to go to work and get off, on the corner.
A figure of speech took the writing down, careful not to tear the tissue.
In love it could be anyone. It could be anyone, in love.
Earthquake glass with instant replay. Aubade. Aubade.
Brotherhood of the sea. The magazine language
of the magazine L=A=N=G=U=A=G=E. Input for the haiku movement.
No restrictions, but only quality work. No sex, violence, or far out poems.
It is a formal argument, far from the tactics I mean currently to employ.
In a way not useful to either of us. Note this kid. In a dither or on a dime
writing writing. Jogs, cotillions, reels, and breakdowns.
Carefree is the official tampon of the U.S. Olympic team. I heard that.
Can you believe the Jehovah Witness came *behind* my house to find me?
It's not all that religious to be a woman. The alternatively lyrical and agitated
character of the piece. I'm Stephen. Matthew. David. You name it. We got it.

Fâché avec la lune. Lectures. Recitals. The popularity of the work
is undoubtedly due to its romantic tone and appealing themes, rather
than the level of skill evidenced in the construction, which is academic,
lacking the remarkable concision and mastery of form typical of his earlier work.
Have Larry play a SOLO. Bob can read a poem. But, of course.
A little art can solve a lot of problems and usually does.
Gee, do you think that's what Mayakovsky meant by a cloud in trousers?
Imagine the most exciting fly cruise of the century and then go ahead
and buy it. The name is a night on bold eavesdrop.
An artist chooses within the objective world according to his own subject,
and is free to bend, break, or alter any line that passes before her eye.
There is a tension that exists between depth and surface, which is expressive.
Torture the canvas until it gives up; you taught me to wash my SPONGES.
Now we're with all, Diamanda comes out of the piano onto eager emotional turf.
So it's time to blow the gutteral and aggravate the menacing again.

Is and when he comes to the door to get some more cologne he is just like a pane of glass
Frank O'Hara's longest line? At any rate, a very palpable hat has at you.
Let's go see, what this is all about, our sometime listener, now our scene.
Psycho was cuckoo, but did anyone blame Alfred Hitchcock? Why didn't they
picket all those films butchering womanhood? It's chauvinist conscience and bears
the relation to political protest that cruising does to longing. You know people
are looking for a vehicle. You know TV is *the* inherently lousy medium.
Ira Gershwin's lyrics for *I Can't Believe My Eyes.* A person
who has lost contact with the purpose of their act. The pain's to blame.
There seem to be rules demanding that women sacrifice themselves, when
they are the core of the M-19 movement, and stand by ARMED and amorous.
Build a wall around the self and don't go in. On Sundays,
happy on the bus and at the flea market, spend a little.
At least one of us was supposed to be a doctor, or marry one. Something happened.
Jealousy is not the fear of losing, but of dividing. An imperialist passion.

The first night his dinghy made port Dr. Demento was speaking
of recreational community nudity. He ate the loaf of bread, after school.
The way they often treat each other over men has never inspired my admiration.
Aztec beefcake. Joy Luck. Some trees. As it were, worried.
Look at Hope still raking in the bucks, when he could be shovelling the snow.
The dopey effect of the third person. Mallarmé's alarm.
Verlaine's revolver. It would be good both going and boing boing.
Nobody's going to be famous anymore, except the infamous. Great but unspoke.
With these here duly assembled there are resemblances.
Splendidly bogus training. Chair repair. Van modification.
It was in the book, so to speak. Lists keep track. *Bête chance.*
One way to write one way is to substitute a period for every comma.
Many of the ROWS are exact retrogrades of earlier rows,
bright and hot and mean and gigantically tiny.
People *will* talk. People will say we're in love.

Rewrite the last chapter of November, for it is too dim witted and autumnal.
I remember well the well where was the water.
Black Mountain Springs. No way to saw sawdust, but with a brush.
In Flagstaff on tremendous Saturday, pears are served.
Stop thinking at the first ellipsis. Everlasting red
in the names of mountains. In the last of the great stations,
the sterilizer in the john. As long as the family can stand it.
You kids, are the numbers getting smaller or bigger?
If you don't shut up, I'll turn the light off.
It was a random trip. Nothing was biting. A bit was tandem.
The UNIVERSE is swallowing us. We're in the observation car.
The train is following. We're far away.
I see the ocean. It's waving. This is our train.
The surf is facing up. They're making a house. Still, the engine comes.
They own the lobby. But they can't pick up the tab. We've got the writing.

He put his fingers in her coffee and so became a galley slave.
Think how many countless plants die a day. Think
of the sea as the place where the land is inflated from.
The mirror is made and then will fade. As from the bag we ET.
This is where I get off. Give me life or give me a transfer, tonight.
What you must confuse in your career is direct onslaught
and continual retirement. Scotch, the harried vote.
How think anything else of a person who laughs alot?
The transcendental mental patient, with train tracks at the mouth.
Selected because we heard from passengers. The insufficient illusion
of being present, tense. Hence, oblique sentences to teach the deaf.
A valet of poetry of only palpable intent. Who cut the lines with a razor.
Ma milk can kill you. Trying to establish hisself as a individual.
Omit to eat at tea time. No cheese in the hilt. Turkey for the hostages.
Thinking makes it. You ask SO? But you are wrong.

From the benches of a turned cloud somebody's bosom says go.
Sunup, sunset, nothing other. Yet in the night, all over again.
The bone is back. The period ended. The lower jaw leaves first.
The only thing comparable to words is flesh. It emits them,
surrounds them, and into your head you pour the spirits,
turning grey. Regretting getting older mistakes the soul
of the thing. Hit me, darling. I'd rather be taken in a fit of hiccups.
Acres of scallions above the fruit. We think of Ladysmith in the snow.
Morris' CODE. A mandate without stickum. A soldier without a WAC.
Ouch. I think I'll put that in the Mobile Home News.
Weave not, wanton. The green horn running the red light
goes to traffic school at night. This is the modern auto.
There is the turf, obtuse and scalene. Give my regards to the mess.
It's cake complicated, don't you drink? Oh fuck off, drip.
Why don't you dig a hole in your back yard and stick some wheat in it.

Who could know the kielbasa did not extend to the end of the bun?
His sentence came and got him. He ate it. It was in the bag.
Reeling through each other's hedges, seeking a runner on a split trip.
Stetson mounts substitute for daughter. Daily toils. Ersatz doilies.
Abalone salad at the station. Dallas in Alabama. Paper money only as good
as the latest reigning ERROR. A sweathog with shaved underarms.
The baby's snot is "caked" on its face. Running down, its yellow rheum.
Everything is up to date in Kansas City. How stressed is your tale?
Either way one of the gay sisters. Note this. In a scale of one to ten
he was a cat with no life left. But her bed dictated *apartheid*.
Drinks alcohol. Courts sentencing. Deft in the hallway and daft on the porch.
Now, would killer wolves aid Alaska moose more? Old Tolstoy's yellow weather.
The maintains its prowess, like Joliet, as it wore a complete sentence.
And ore keeps getting away from you, so you exercise the abandoned mind.
I don't know otherwise why you would want to get down, in an armored chair.

A beaver with a hardon. Think Print. The mind's flaccid pitcher. Ink Friendship.
The salvos of P.E.N. members. Promise us you won't be promiscuous,
semi-gloss demimonde. Her knees smiled up at me under their a...HEM.
Punctuation is only mortal. Okay to exclaim a few times before expiring.
Love to fuck in t-shirts. Jack the Ripper's veil of tears. One *t* loves another.
Serial acid. Weed made his paranoia paranoid. What I need is a benny.
Genteel mothballs. New shingles for the academy cottage. Spinach
in a white sauce. Onion tears on's cheek. On the other HAND
he's not going to hurt anyone, though he does own a pea shooter.
They're both potheads from number go. Rigor mortis bars barrettes.
More pork barrel back scratch in house his 'n her programming.
Lice in her blouse. A clasp or bar for holding a woman's hair in place.
It was all up in the air. Too scared to come. Frightened of leaving.
A couple of good lines about what she's been doing as a PROOF reader.
Meanwhile, back on earth, the bookstore owner, friend of poetry and of libraries.

So lying forward weakly on the handrail, I had to own sometimes
I could see nothing but lilacs and endless rock. Bless those who croak
for Croatian independence. I'm going out riding on the ocean.
Without war there would never be draft. This was a hard blow
to swallow, but it kept the ship AIRBORNE, and besides the fucker was strong.
That cat embarking up the wrong tree. A yoyo situation but still a horse race.
Pomulus tremuloides, shaking as pens. Penny's lulu birdland out of town.
The hitch. The turd will disappear, the tissue will not. Oars. Ours.
Hutch. Sobek. Leave not a match behind. And I'll not
ask for chapstick. These were the notations from tableland.
Did you give her the incentive yet? We just aren't interested
in another human interest story, so get up there in front of that BACKDROP.
This is the age in which you set yourself the task of learning
to rebuild the car you feel the necessity not to drive.
A kitchen is fluff. A blanket is frosting. And so, the night is over again.

There's a new dyke in town. The ring the bride wears in the tub
to avoid being nothing more than just another person who loves it.
A hopeless parody of shit. That brother over there wearin' a nice pair.
Piña colada hatred. A scabies spot. Bankrupt Liquors.
Able neither to hold on nor to let go. All other fish SOURCES
inaccessible, till somebody slays what was coming along just anyway.
One SATURATION job (it might take how long?) and you're in forever.
A, in fact, it's gas. The goal. A hunk with a horn.
As he throws his wrap on the floor, loaded, William Carlos Williams like
his great predecessor Whitman includes all human qualities with the addition
of one, and that is *nastiness*; by virtue of its almost total absence in Whitman's work
there follows an actual fault therein present: too much enthusiasm.
Sometimes frank, but it's amusing. "Tall buildings." "Small change."
Thy will be done. Easter is good to travellers, so there. Blah, blah, blah.
The spine is sewn. The most expensive part of any new construction is the plumbing.

We portage anyway. (Canoes.) The only toilet paper is your own.
We're the 84 Rooms. You can't afford it. You can't offend it.
The city ablaze with combinations of the L shaped world.
It's the same thing every day. No program but a skiagraph: a SKOGRAM.
Beyond the lines of the here, to, for. Liszt kept track. The queer swallows come
to Capistrano and back. I'll say. You sent me. Pigpen. Deciduous grown.
We'll say anything, so everything is said. The body made it up. The mind behind.
Something happens. Somebody is supposed to doctor, playing on the wagon.
Smoke aside, verbs ate him. Yeats' Hoolihan, beating her breast again.
I am that blood spattered brain what AIMS. Do you like any of the other
candidates? My word man. Return Puerto Rico to the Indians.
Is that nugget loaded? Tiny periods of infant aporea. Like as not.
Where between your shop and your digestion lies your heart?
Some shit is some times edible, depending on your family.
We have no art. We'll sell anything, complete with Slavonic feelings.

So I'm at the Gift Wrap counter of the La Jolla Sears to buy a World Airways ticket
and the clerk picks up the phone and says, "Water heaters."
Long before the poem, I knew I was a poet. Riding up 7 to Wheeling
in the car. You don't play gambling, you've got a game in your belly.
Three quarters of the time most people don't show up. Turn it down.
Time is the tempest. We've been through this a hundred times before.
Four storey winds. All the things that will not CHANGE.
And when you woke, you cried to dream again. Miserable food,
all you do is prolong flight. And dying, the old draw life
from a cigarette. SAP CHECK. Yourself the foe. Till husbands.
Adore the son. The baby perceived the bees as *eating* the flowers.
And so they were. The body is the frame. The machine is connected to the mouth
by a pin. By night the mind, by day the limbs. ROOF to ruinate.
Acceptable audit. And then a last call from Loco Grande, the alcoholic gardener
of the house: you were good to me, although it was a mirage.

We all await an idiot's judgment. You can't afford to wait.
You can't afford not to wait. Penelope *is* the journey she had to offer.
If you had any sense you would treat everything as though it were a thread.
The jingoists are going to have to learn the hardest ways. Rain is the sister
of decay. I despise your interminable versified troubles. I reject
everything popular. Let me hip you to the SEAMS. My bicycle put me here.
That's where the English is, asking how Spanish Spain could be now.
He was just about the only decent conventional poet around, as far as he could see.
He knew when a man signed on to be President, behind that dollar was the end.
The artist's eternal chinos; the fuchsia in the whiffle ball; Sam
Francisco; the Mom and Pop arab grocery in the Mission; the northernmost doorperson
on the upper east side. And with love you boxed, for it was the loosener of limbs.
May we stop this senseless REDNESS? My clouds are tainted but lovingly puffed,
and I daresay Denver *is* lonesome, for her heroes. So Anthony says bye
to Alexandria, and we are swiftly inside, the resurrection accomplished *again*.

Let me at some other date show you what it is. Your reputation rises
when you die. Want to see me make a circle with a Y in it?
Take care. It is very clumsy. Don't dribble on the court like an old man.
Fish TIPPLE in the deep. You get thin. I knew you as a chubby fucker,
isolated from the avant garde, making your way back to pictographs.
I think of Tom as a clear-cut example of himself and it doesn't confuse me.
I try to come to that realization about everything. Don't get carried away
in your craft. Take the elevator. You have to get into it.
Some cats be walkin' on a path of jam. A gigolo on the go,
demanding it in his FLYING BOA. So Sunday night is always a problem.
If you have to think of doctors, inventors, and social reformers, think of Joseph
Ignace Guillotin. A considerable part of his business was the resort trade. Now,
I would like to know about the purple shield cash funeral plan and receive my free
thermometer. The devastation will make this area a tourist attraction big as Grand Canyon.
You still hang out. It is very chummy. The bathroom smells like a nursery.

How you roar in that room. How you yawn. Couple more hours
and this place be just like Chicago. He breathe on something and it
turn rosé. So wear furry boots and stand in the corner of the yard.
Next time we'll paint the town red. No green or they'll think
it's a landscape. We all know this to be a banquet of knowledge to begin with,
protected by bulkheads. And I wanted to be an accepted fucking MASON.
The trouble with any moral ambition in a writer is that the truth is so
demoralizing, one is lucky to survive telling it at all. White
liquidates milk. What's a highsmith? clam dregs and vodka. My body lies
over the ocean. Not to display emotion in the face of extinction is mentally unbalanced.
The wine marketeer dies red. My belly trembles like leaves, blowing into Paris.
A long wandering in the orient is what one deserves in later life. The only happiness
is to be shut up in art. The only casualty, not escaping insufferable events. The night
is soft and warm, if you can live with a head up your sleeve. I want to cause you
nothing but insight and pleasure. You must excuse me. I have to go and do my reed work.

Plastic Sutures

                              As the sluice
pours forth its granular flayings a new cloud rises
and interplanetary driftings become simply initiatory gifts
like the circumcision of a black horse. I yield up
my lover to the reveries, completely, until he is taken away
by the demons who then deliver me their BOLTS *from afar*
like drunken Magi.

                              I have
Only my intermittent life in your thoughts to live
Which is like thinking in another language. Everything
Depends on whether somebody reminds you of me...
It's not the incomplete importunes, but the spookiness
Of the finished product...since ALL
By definition is completeness.

Plastic Sutures

The modern battlefield is dense with signals. Most of them will be decoys
to fool the other side. But we are trying to harden our true signals.
We call this ERADCOM, feeling fat, keeping warm, paying our debt to the Tartars.
We live here and we have absolutely no feeling of nationalism,
and once we were so susceptible we could have been parted by the wind.
There is nothing to mount but the bluff. I dreamt there was this shit house,
with big tubs where the shit was. Above these were roasts being cured.
You dig the density of material thought. Without material no one can be said
to have a lead at all, and the world is a giant simultaneous performance
of numerous unfamiliar, but fucking, actions. Count them. We are united
in art as others are united in faith, in crime, in alcohol, in political ambition.
Editors change Paris. There are many artists without much art. What we want is poetry
without poets. So the reason I forget names is the moment you remember them
you are no longer in touch with what is before you. What I am looking for
in a reader is a certain amount of misunderstanding of what is happening.

Hello, Mummy, you look lovely in there. I don't know who I am. The mung beans
are a supple lifeline that puts my skin in jeopardy. Putting on my jeans
doesn't mean I have to take off my fortune, does it? But if you want your seven bucks,
we're going to have to go out to Venice and take Lewis off. Look, there has never been
a new wave. Five minutes at any shore should satisfy the most doubtful idiot
on this point. The idea predates PARACELSUS, and is original shit.
Death as the mother of beauty has decay reform what is degenerate
into something new and perfectly great. You understand that
true actual syntax is musical, but as formal as the stroke of a painter.
We are all equally alive, therefore wrong. We create the world
in a horizontal bed of light. The woman made paintings of dancers and paintings
to be worn by dancers. She painted her CAR.
Underneath her painting was a body, dancing to Michael Palmer.
I'm on the brink of the edge of the razor. If you want to know what is
happening, become a monthly member. The feeling part is almost over.

Oh bad! oh bad! Little Jesus rock on lower Sproul.
I spend all day in the library, while I am in the world.
I am the manager, the bookkeeper, the bass player, the vocalist, the chauffeur,
and the backer of this band. I went to see the Gang of Four at the American
Indian Center, you know. That was the Bay of Pigs. These are the B People.
The Byproducts of Berkeley go crazy, and all I can hold is the telephone.
Hello you're on the air. I'm on the air and . . . the fucking tree
has birds in its hair. Doesn't LAMINATED just feel like a lamb in the fields?
"A mild game to divert the doorperson and we are swiftly inside."
I haven't been getting much sleep. When I'm away from home,
I'm in the library. When I'm home, I'm in the library.
We make a world something like the brain and there is something in the brain
that isn't right. Are the cherry seedlings safe from the rabbits? Or the Kerouac Dynasty's
Rocky Mountain summer school? You know technique is *always* a means of arriving
at a statement. If you look at a rock long enough, you become sub-rock.

More of the slung leg motif. I knows what you means.
If you've had a accident, marriage or divorce problem, need a will,
or are just looking for a cerebral Robert Redford, this is the end of the curve.
I care, about how long, the crack is. Everything is based on beer.
And it's not sentimental, because when he's speaking of himself he's speaking of you
and he is on a cloud. I didn't keep a notebook until I thought
you could compose in your sleep. Fifty dollars worth of groceries in one bag,
with one banana in it. It *is* difficult to be obsessed with phonemes. Commitment to form
is often commitment to the status quo. It preserves class. Those interested in change
change the content. Here it dips. All we can safely say of the author
is that we do not know who he was or where he lived or when he wrote.
His excellence and influence are matters of more importance.
The areas of loss are filled with GESSO and smoothed to conform
to the surrounding paint, then varnished before inpainting can occur.
I don't complain. Well, I complain all the time. But I can't complain.

I come from a house of at least fifty birds, receiving disgraceful fortune
cookie crumbles. B tells me I should have bought orange juice
futures last year. Does he take me for an interloper?
Filled with divine afflatus? Grandeur without intensity?
A porker in tears. But not yet have I blown the noble strain,
although it is his birthday. Not a single emotion but a whole congress,
though the diction stamps danger in its FIGURE. Now it was evening, etc.
Bell ringing was too often pretentious, for us to pretend it.
The animal most of all who looked only at the dinner table was the cow.
Tumors are evil things, whether in bodies or in books. And her napkins were marvels.
Given the world, you should develop your faculty for stomaching.
The most effective figure will be that which is undisclosed.
He cut himself into strips until he made mincemeat of himself and disappeared.
On the other hand speed is in season. When you have passed through the place you now are,
you will board a ship and reach a great city. But it will not be Spring.

I smell of what we drink that is a root. I see the stones along the fence of school.
I taste the mess of which we put at lunch. I hear I am confused of it.
Pencilmen eat more cuttlefish. If your lips ache, change your embouchure.
Lady, your tennis shoes are glowing. The name of the work is DIE.
It's hard to tell which heads are becoming and which are decaying.
Some decay can be becoming, if you know what I means.
A five minute EPOXY frisbee prosthesis. No music, but zinc and quince and gore.
You walk into a Soho gallery and you might see a pile of butter neatly sculpted in the corner.
Three days later you go back and it has been spread around the gallery with a scythe.
If it's not your house, it's your subway. Ghoul candies by Rodney Ripps.
Radon daughter. The woman checking out her hickey in the reflection of Cartier's window.
Nolde tried to be a Nazi, but they rejected him. Motherwell hangs his canvasses
between his own Matisses, to see if they look okay. Nice work if you can get it.
Do you feel good about your body? The best way to understand cubist distortion
of the human face, is to keep your eyes open when you're making it.

Well, the fruit breeding tests are over. Now what? Let's have a quaalude orgy.
Let's go AER LINGUS. Let's get sleepy and fuck. People want you to run into them.
When you can't tell whether someone is gay or just well dressed, you know you're in
a fancy part of town. If a man's pants fit well on the other hand, you know he's not
interested in you. It ain't me, Bruce, it's the okra. He's a complete asshole I know,
but he's on the board of the Carnegie Foundation and I don't want him sent a lawyer's letter!
Nobody makes salmon icing like Willem de Kooning. Who *were* the two disciples of Buddha?
The woodpeckers are mating and squabbling, seeing there is no need for security.
And we are becoming degenerate, before we are mature. The racketeers have captured
our gullible minds. Better to err on the side of generosity, than anal retention.
In Rome I spent all my time watching Westerns in a moviehouse near the Vatican.
My favorite dish was MOO GOO GAI PAN. We met everyday at the caviarteria. Sea robins.
Think tanks. They all made large and self-important work out of a notion of trash.
I realized when they got famous that my own work was a time bomb. Change edits Paris.
But I love oranges and asses too much to ever rise more than a tower or two above them.

I'm coming over someday unannounced for some of your evening primrose root soup.
Having a distinct attraction to melancholy lyrics didn't prevent Grieg from pouring
his richness across the Norwegian sky. I don't do it like that. I just bite it plain.
It's getting so hairy I don't even have the nerve anymore to sneak onto the fucking train.
Now, the squeegee for the shower door is in the Master bath, under the sink.
If a beachhead of cooperation can push back a jungle of suspicion, you strive
for the loose and casual look of the unemployed. Phoenician protection is a requirement.
There weren't always imitation bacon bits, and as you know $7.95 is too much for paper
back poetry. Are these "seeds aboil in CELLS of night?" Asphyxiated but not yet embalmed,
they survive, drinking quinine and ipecac. Nothing so bad as ordinary sweet and sour sauce.
And sperm was cheap, but this one had gap teeth and walked with a gimp.
He walked through the valley of the shadow of death scared of nothing,
except possibly an educated fingernail. They were terrible in their language.
Flowers wilt and rose, and wouldn't you know, the Prince of Madagascar dropped his fly,
saying I bathe that others may breathe. I don't care who makes me come. Jim Brodey takes a bath.

Cachoo. Cachooie! He was an omnivorous cat for all things editable.
He entered the world with his mother's I.U.D. in his hand.
Not just another cheap little version of the avatar starving. Too late to be late,
but earlier than expected. Louis the Wideawake. Louis the Bruiser.
It is a sobering thought to realize that even a dear friend can recoil
from the mere act of your veriest presence. But you are ready, like a javelin.
Love's GEYSER sprays the camping hordes with punctuality and its spermacidal tales
of lithesome night. In short, *tu* in person. She went all gaga for your creased pants.
The tumult rose, an airy crotch beside the deep, and we got sick.
The travail of this condition only partly damns you, and having nothing
else to do you depart. The going out is arduous, but you are hard
and wet and there. There are of course cow pies, dust bunnies, road apples.
Then, far from the rabid hawk and leanto, the dam you made floats movingly to sea,
deep below the plains of southern France, like a goose at the first stop for grass.
In a word, the first educated white person to have seen the Mississippi and could write.

Listen, Hortense, forget it. If I am telling you something you should stop listening
only because you are. Proceed without comparison. These are hard works.
It's useless to examine what is still living. *Salsipuedes.* You don't know
what you are missing. Get out of your car. John Coltrane started playing clarinet
in school. Have you been to the Judy Chagall? Cy Twombly hits the big time
just when the fashion world discovers twenty shades of beige. Agnes Martin
wir lieben. Diebenkorn learnt it from Schwitters and Matisse, Katz from Porter and Avery.
No one can ever be more than just another supreme idiot in the river.
Anything else is just a delusion to encourage professionalism or commerce.
It is a mistake to refer to artists by their first names, unless they are in the room.
"Painters paint, they don't teach," he yelled, at the top of his voice.
I like the frames better than the paintings. I wonder what the man is doing on the CAN
this year. He puts titles on to prove he has a mind. The school of spaghetti.
He couldn't come through a shower curtain. What we are after in art is cover—
intricacy and obsession all-over. For deep into death, blacks look red.

A large flower in a woman's hair is a comparison.
The first thing to do on the way to an artistic career is to learn how to make
a frame up. Take an international airport and hang a begonia at the information desk.
Say "for tortuga" to the clerk. Modesty and seriousness are such important lessons to learn
that sometimes it must appear you haven't learnt them. ¡Malcolm Morley!
A woman with a mouth for a necklace and a scalpel for a bike, loving
all that Afro-American art music we call jazz. LOCAL yokels,
looking after the LEGENDS. How did they meet? She went to this orgy
and saw his picture. He worked for the Whole Earth Truck Store and has a good body.
It was cinchy and fun, in her eurythmic shoes. I got my moccies on.
To bid the galley do. Her *wheat*, her *wheat*, her *wheat*!
If it's not the radio, it's the record player. It's liberty, polemic, and the Housatonic
at the B.P.O.E. You slow Charlie Parker down and it sounds like Lester Young.
Novelists *have* to be paid more, because what they do isn't worth as much.
If you'll come and see me and take my part, needless to say I'll love you, needlessly.

The jewels are so that we may fuck. I'm not mad. I'm just mad at you.
This country conned Minerva out of her spirit in 1781. The first American OPERA
was written by a Declaration of Independence signee. Water evaporating
from a continuous sea. Oblivious green mesa. Increase substance
and make the eventuality inevitable. Tragedy is passion, but experience is comedic.
If you don't cough up, we're going to etiolate the leaves. Bar None.
A week's vacation on the Riviera is no longer more expensive than a night in the hospital.
I think I caught one of those contiguity disorders going around. The French
suck on chic uniformity. Marseilles was already settled in Sappho's time.
Corinna taught Pindar a thing or two. The only good poem is the one that's read.
The roommates in the ordinary language school. Bird's cancelled trip with Edgar Varèse.
We consume more packaging than product. Don't you think *Dishonoured* is the great
von Sternberg Dietrich vehicle, not *Der Blaue Engel*? The only man made thing
visible from the moon is the Great Wall of China, and Mao was born on Christmas.
And I'm probably the only person in the world to know exactly what that thing over there is.

Want to go to some nursery and look at STRAIGHTJACKETS? The green alligator that you love
was the world. Everyone is stuck with being themselves. A non-musician devotee
of swing—in short, a mammoth who has the cheek to call Robert Duncan a hoax
to his eye. From the Vince Lombardi Service Area on the Jersey Pike at night,
it's cars. The Nineties are coming, a humoresque, and all you have to do is hurry.
Don't drink from the tap. You who were prepared by your founder to be a prisoner.
A law is a way to delay an attack. "The kinda coon he wanna become
exclude the kinda pickaninny she be." America already sacrificed its best
early poet to Napoleon. One touch of difference, racism.
Great deal of difference, harmony. Kim Chi Ha. Dioxin in the swimming pool.
Plutonium in the fridge. Before technology there were no accidents. Eskimos bathed in urine
because of the temperature. The fetching innuendo of bamboo
in the snow. Or my great great grandfather Onward and his nameless wife.
She was a three speed with a bell and no kick stand. Mechanical American
chainlink lunacy in the corridor. Impervious Artaud-like obsession on the bench.

For my part I want either a reconstituted tongue or received knowledge.
Could Berg's First Piano Sonata be the most impressive Opus 1 ever created?
Every phrase seems predestined in Bing Crosby's *Let's Fall In Love*.
Isn't Harold Alden's *When We Were Young* better than any of Beethoven's vocals?
The eyebrows will never forgive us. I don't care, so long as I can arrive at some neck
of the woods in the nick of time. Everyone knows M and N are the only letters
that should make your nose vibrate. We met on a retreat. Suckling and Lovelace
were his favorite poets. You could see for yourself the spent purpose
of a perfectly bent penis. I was the tape when he won the race.
Oh well, if you ever need a chair, it's on the plaza. We are our ancestors,
and we are our unborn. One could do worse than sit down and observe what is passing.
Ordinary human love can RUIN a being for the experience of real love. This is best
accomplished from a bench. You come to realize that love without shakti is mush.
Besides, it's hard to forget someone when there's always a picture around somewhere.
The ease of the ocean when it reaches the shore is lost on such people.

In Hawaii the flowers are so beautiful it almost eases the pain of what has been
done there. Father's Day, or Bloomsday. Just so it leads to another jacquerie.
John Trudell's family, born on Alcatraz, was later burned to death by this country's
bureau of investigation. I love the way people I love devise to keep going.
But cancel my subscription to the tricentennial. No revolution gets two bills.
Investigate the disservice matches do to our interest in fire. Subterfuge may be
the respectable technique. The weak write strong music. ART likes deformity.
Cf. Percy Grainger's defense of flagellation. I prefer whole cloth to most
coherently contrived intention, which stakes its claim to the bowels of the earth.
I am an archaeologist in the archive of everything now. You are moving toward a box
or a flame—to be shoved downward or go out. There is nothing to own but up.
If you are not here, why don't you leave? Go germinate your own crop.
There are less flowers in the world than there used to be. This is measurable
by the size of the world honey crop. If bees be less, then so are we.
With the eyes of a saint and the perceptions of a ghost, we have galoshes up to our eyebrows.

Is it time now to consider the music of Mongo Santamaria?
I wish I were one with my poem. No one knew if it was any good.
Because he read it so well no one could tell. He was trying to impress his friends,
the men. How can anyone who goes have nothing to say? Let's BOOK.
Yet how tentatively people enter a new restaurant for the first time,
blinded by the stress and losing the immunity of yesteryear. It was snowing,
a Maine-eating seaboard. Active ingredient pure talc. Paris edits change.
Could SEMEN be considered a dairy product? It was to be his *On A Girdle*.
Form was the mother, the former mater, the Latin for mother.
The reassurance of a growing penis. Atlanta lemurs nothing.
Women who hate men so much they are unable to speak to them.
An astringent iced tea concoction. An honest attempt to furnish a room with thin air.
Past a certain empty field the hike is done. In a truck I dream I am on a bus.
Just because Carl Jung saw a pile of shit in the corner of his room
when he was young, doesn't mean we shouldn't just relax a little.

The sound a slide projector makes between slides is the closest approximation
of swallowing that it can do. It doesn't matter who said it.
Look to your satrap and buy on the margin. This is my writing.
Let's saponify the info for the purpose of catharsis. It's raining in my ears.
It feels like raining in my ears. A dark, tossed Sargasso salad,
peppered with violets. My accent is something finer than could be purchased
in so removed a dwelling as your own. Joan, Margaret, Joan, Ann,
Gilbert, Edmund, Susanna, Judith, and Rik. *Bas chevet*. No?
Waves break night's watch. Sleeping in cars, age is just another form.
Vivaldi was the director of the Venice girls choir. And Harvard is not enough.
This is bovine wilderness we call homa. Taylor Mead is our Noel Coward.
Steve Benson our Stan Laurel. Nemo Coin. Spotswood Green. Big John Wilkes.
The ORANGERY TYPETTE. The great Lafayette Leak. So cop and how
if you could just put your hand on that there suzerain *thang!*
you would be a pompadour amidship, or a contemptible stumblebum on a flagpole.

M, O, A, I, doth sway my life. Her C's her V's and her T's.
Is this a poem of practise or will you be a thing in lingo? I agree.
Next up Fabian, Belch, then Curio as clean-up.
That which exists through me is called extra innings.
Perception is fatal. Daylight and champion. Life were nothing but an exercise
in breathing. Prince Zen, face the musicians. There's a crisis afoot.
Couldn't we bury the hatchet? It could be all pigses. War?
Where? Good snood. Do birds have art? or do they just sing what comes
to mind. Watch out or you'll bear the same relation to that that Kenneth
Rexroth does to jazz. Make yourself a baby and hold it, for you don't stand
a chance with a ghost like your *self*. Ants love marijuana in Oakland.
Ashtray is piglatin for trash. I dedicate my work to the study of the OTHER.
I want you to have the yacht. Few things in poetry are more essentially repulsive
than someone reciting it. Some kind of funky swan. Some sort of Arizona
surf machine. Some Shrubbery. What we knew when we were you know where.

WE DYE SHAG, Let's hope snow for the kid. An Xmas globule.
When I see you it makes me want to be a shut-in.
You and your 700 fussy tailors, and all her help wears handkerchiefs.
I extend to you a fratricide's hand. They've got bad manners
and boring morals, we'll just have to assess a penalty.
Henrietta Westerly and her little felony. All the bunk and boohoo of what is.
The whole hostage thing is just having a drink with Ptolemy.
A helicopter napalming the heliotropic is an American invention.
Now, one only partly British Isle. A bad SEAHOG at Greenwich Mean Time.
If we had an Irishman who needed to be paid to fight the English, we'd assassinate him.
We'll hancock the Star Island agreement, so long as the turns are met.
Homosexuality requires enlightenment. The G-40 Plus Club for slightly older gays.
Midnight amity under the direction of the aurodrama. Lorcan hillsides.
Musical barbarians. Speedboat this morning. Then come the mice to meet you.
A five year old boy, standing guard at the door of his lesbian mother.

The French know *cloud* without an ascender, imagine that.
Wooden words, like a paroled con, manipulate the process
with a design of their own. A tree is nothing but the air's kite.
Art cannot correct what technology has mistook. An edition of *Finnegan's Wake*
without a typo would be unthinkable. But does the ruler of heaven listen
to this stuttering? Perhaps it *is* just nature's way of keeping everything
from happening at once. Her way of telling us to spend money.
Gin and icicles. Sporting and military chocolate. I need my morning LINE!
A field of hideous blonde six year old soccer stars. Too much gulf.
Not enough dread. Ashley ashes destroy Datsun but *hush.*
A nubbin fossil in the turf. A tuumba without a hand.
A frisky consensus of three. Russia bound corn from Iowa.
The coroner's coronary. A jewel on his pinkie. Morman jive and tackle.
Mahler in the tabernacle. John's piece *The Heavens Shall Glow Beyond*
for prepared earth. His weltanschauung was finished.

This is done in arch form: 2-5, 1-4, 3 repeats, etcetera.
If you can't come around, at least you telephone. I don't want any other love.
I hold the leash and hear the water splashing off the tree. The stanza slackens.
The short sentence is change for the dollar you bring to it. My wrap lies
on the steps of the esplanade. A tongue tie. Loosener of limbs. For what is a SONG
but a bastard counterfeit of persuasion? People have been more or less undecided
about wine for the past 3,000 years, but you too can make a few bucks saying Jack
Kerouac, Jack Kerouac. You can have an orgasm in your shoulder or in your neck,
and incredibly they will bring you your car. Deracinated savagery conceived
from observation. Siberia isn't sunny enough, and Afghanistan is about the only place
the Americans haven't put up their hotels. Pass the fagot to bright burning Troy.
Look, we put money in banks and do everything else that people do.
I like to party with friends and then I like to be by myself again.
Boy, was I drunk. Was he handsome. Did my mom give me hell.
I am, that is, the piebald colt of heaven. I only tremble in tropical waters.

I.e. nobody tells me how to play Space Invaders. Henry Kaiser's got his own.
Polycontrast is bad. What we have here is a cross between QUANTUM THEORY
and the UNCERTAINTY PRINCIPLE. There are now more photographs in the world
than there are bricks. The head is in need of a valve job. In deed we find intelligence.
Besides, the muse can't do her job without it. The men against violence toward women
have a dynamite slide show, while in a grave I sat reclined.
This is the B of A crackdown. Refuse to eat on orange seats.
There's an eyelash in your math. Check out Johns' version of Munch's bedspread.
You're supposed to stay AROUND awhile. Who knows for what but you're supposed to
stay here for a while. Eat alot of fruit and do your āsanas, until you are hit.
Drawn shades cover the waterfront. If you listen you will hear
the modern genius everywhere. You're in the V. O. mood. You've got the woman.
You've got the shirt. You're looking at the camera. You're high. You're yellow.
You do what you've gotta do. You have to. You're getting paid.
Now how are we ever going to teach these birds the gospel?

Survivors of debridement, developing pneumonia under emergency burn treatment,
fly the new seven ton American flag. Weighs more than a hundred Betsy Rosses.
Really, who wants to settle for an ad twice a year in the Village Voice.
Tonight's special is Shepherd's Pie. Sword swallowers
take it out back and eat it on a rock. Is real estate really
the ultimate hedge? The only logical reason to own property is to sell it.
I take my money from heiresses. I mess around with dope. Did you ever hear
of someone named LaBont? Well you will. Clifford Brown plays my kind of trumpet,
but nothing like, after a long trip, Dex. Remember all about what you said.
The future's crypt opens wide its doors. They were just roving PROPHYLACTICS
in the Reagan Administration. They were the ones who arranged Rockefeller's death.
Reagan's life. It's high time this country had leadership of celluloid and oil.
In our last chapter the destroyer had tied up at Iceland and the Captain
and executive officer were drunk. Older people, well, their hands shake.
It indicated a decided lack of design savvy to print a poem like *The Skaters* sans serif.

You and I, we have the same typewriter in the Western night, tired at Easter.
It's been a long time since it was true that anything we did was art and it's about time
the shells were dumped out with the eggheads. Mar the clay and score the pot.
Nice to see the colored brothers getting into their latin possibility.
The testy, bean-dip eating winners of prizes. How vulgar can you get?
The girl you're sleeping with would lick the diseased asshole of a CIA agent.
According to Ice Berg Slim, the ex pimp, no person is good when in bed.
How could such a smart man propose such a dumb thesis?
The tokens wore his pockets. Before he left his two month captivity as a hostage,
the U.S. Ambassador kissed a tiny female guerilla who was wearing a blue satin mask.
"She's a doctor," he said. One of those enthusiastic but not extraordinarily
sophisticated sorts that approves too much. So you want to join the bar?
that profession prepossessed with ideas of wrong which invents a notice of justice
as its ideal? What we are developing here is overtakelessness.
No job is really interesting that is not trouble from the start.

You can tell looking at Malevitch why the Russians beat us into space,
and why we followed. Spar integrity in the rotor blade. But nothing so beautiful
as the earth on dope. Bunchberry, loosestrife, hog peanut, common agrimony.
He did alot for the arts, then everybody griped cause he fooled around a little.
He didn't even know death's mother-in-law. Coors beer at the Phantom Ranch.
He wasn't having any of it. He was into Hoop Art. He liked Brice Marden,
the writer. They're beautiful. They're the ones that don't get dirty.
The filly has a little filling in the right hind ankle on the outside,
where there is a nick. She was a phantom of delight when first she raked me over.
I felt like the view the camera had of its shutters. A record is a postcard of MUSIC,
and thought destroys NATURE. The planning commission in India is mounting a cremation
forestry program, putting women to work in rural areas so there'll be enough wood
to burn the dead bodies. Lacking real dead, the merchants hung their flags
at half mast for the hostages, who were as *good* as dead.
Nobody wants to die single, but it's nature makes you go, into the herald air.

Adieu, nice presents. Adieu, unpardonable thingamabob.
You have a rubious lip. You feel the bite as the orgasm
which the mosquito is too small to have within. Treetop tendrils
dovetailing willy nilly. Considerably different, if not altogether opposite,
his hearing did derring-do, though the peerers were sure to veto it.
But it was as SPORT at eventide, and it made his heritage just blossom.
But this is not the sunset and twilight of Bernard Berenson. This is
federal abortion. Exciting things are happening which affect our health.
Long live Rudy Chapa. They plan to inseminate an elephant with elephantine sperm,
doctored to contain the genes of the long extinct wooly mammoth,
and they plan to do this in Michigan, where G.M. executives are selling their stock.
They're no dummies. I am. A notion that decays almost the moment is is plucked,
like a lute stop. In one sense and out the other. Might it be a budding schizoid,
experiencing this thing called father hunger? A city's architecture *is* a collage.
A cut-up is an autopsy. I didn't study examples, but lacked none.

Whatever you think, this life is devoted to out and out seriousness.
I have nothing to say but health and activity to you all. And thanks to Goya,
and to Billy Strayhorn. All this was but a camisado. Put up your dukes.
Love is not a gift, but an achievement. Otherwise, carless people full of smoke.
Stone or bone. The rich imitate the garb of the out of work in self defense.
I saw a man meticulously picking for ten resolute minutes through the garbage can
at the bus stop, surrounded by people with money. He drank the end of the coke cup.
He took out the newspapers. He rescued the aluminum. I joined the INFANTRY
to finish my education and get some muscles and put enough bread together
to buy a motorcycle, going where the women are veiled and a guy with a trained moth
could make a fortune. I never dreamed of being a cable splicer
when I was a little girl. I don't think you need any color yet, but we should start
thinking about it. The first greying sometimes arrives
before the acme's reached. Waxy sisal. Ghastly pudding. You moan,
you squirm, you scream, you rope, you tie me. Shop Talk.

I'm tossing nature at your feet and you fret about the shit on your chaussures.
Intention is to write as though the language were predestined. Eventually you end
up on some rock, talking to your jailer. I've had enough evening already.
But there is a delicate FORM of the empirical which identifies itself so intensely
with its object that it thereby becomes a theory. Visible are the burning dollars
in the knowledgable red night. Home from the war, the war at home.
Music is, after all, the only importance this country can claim in the world at large.
So I'm going to be furious when you grow up without me, writing your Ode to Sport,
breakfasting sine croissants, putting down roots in astroturf. It is you know
not I. It is an image of what I do, that's all folk. I know the people
I have believed, and I am persuaded they can keep what has been delivered.
Hola, meshuggeneh. Ciao, bistecchina. The theme is not to X the stream.
Hold fast the form of sound words. Let the SPLEEN be the correction of the intestines.
In extreme, the spirit that survives destruction. But I didn't just get dropped here.
I made my way. It is too late for argument. Look. The long walk has already begun.

Codex

That is the glebe and this is the glissando. The future is nothing
But a flying wing. You must make your case either with names or with an unfolding.
A position or a disclosure, a microbus. The corridor, the cascade, what stuck.
Glacier notes over the tops of hills. To be close again, as it was in the leanto.
Lengthen the line and increase the leading. These are the helloes of progress.
At the kitchen table the books are pored over, much as a neighbor will bum a cigaret.
The bungalow, radioed and occupied, has no other path to follow but the venture,
The undeniable yielding turmoil mapped out for us for life.
Somebody might ought cook someone a square meal. Life in our adulthood
Is mistaken for wanting completion.What it longs to do is continue being.
The BEES are sleeping beneath the pergola. At the end of each lesson is the vocabulary.
If one opening clouds, another will clear, so long as you both will breathe.
Where's a shovel or something, I say, what can dig, or a trowel? Language pointed
To its content. A crowd of people at the beach screaming "Tuna! tuna!" The evening
Breeze, trembling trees, the night, the stars. And there you are, in a manner of speaking.

So at sunset the clouds went nuts. They thought they were a text.
This language of the general o'erflows the measure, but my brother and I liked it alot.
I think I'll just pause long enough here to call God a bitter name.
Ripeness is all right but the lip is a couplet and nobody knows fuck-all about it.
The THREAD has always been bias. There are alternatives to purchasing goods
To recruit admirers. Right, but is it what Verdi would have wanted?
Nor is it enough to be seen by your youngers as having carried the tradition
To a good place. Given disasters everywhere, don't drink from the tap.
And for what reason make anything that is not for flight?
There are treatments to keep your retina from becoming detached but for what—
To see this? Why, there are things about Israel not dreamed of in the Bible.
How could I miss you when my aim is dead. The goal is sea sounds not yet writ.
All right. Enjoy the heads of your beaches. I'm not going in order
To get tied up on spec, but I wanted you to meet your fellow brains. Thank you,
People of destiny, for your brilliant corners. I like your voice. Look where it's come from.

Index

DANTE ALIGHIERI THE NEW LIFE
Translated by Dante Gabriel Rossetti; Preface by Michael Palmer

ANDRÉ BRETON AND PHILIPPE SOUPAULT THE MAGNETIC FIELDS
Translated by Charlotte Mandel

PAUL CELAN LETTERS TO GISÈLE
Translated by Jason Kavett

AMIT CHAUDHURI Sweet Shop: New and Selected Poems, 1985–202

FARNOOSH FATHI GRANNY CLOUD

BENJAMIN FONDANE CINEPOEMS AND OTHERS
Edited by Leonard Schwartz

W. S. GRAHAM *Selected by Michael Hofmann*

SAKUTARŌ HAGIWARA CAT TOWN
Translated by Hiroaki Sato

MIGUEL HERNÁNDEZ *Selected and translated by Don Share*

OSIP MANDELSTAM VORONEZH NOTEBOOKS
Translated by Andrew Davis

HENRI MICHAUX A CERTAIN PLUME
Translated by Richard Sieburth; Preface by Lawrence Durrell

MELISSA MONROE MEDUSA BEACH

VIVEK NARAYANAN AFTER

SILVINA OCAMPO *Selected and translated by Jason Weiss*

EUGENE OSTASHEVSKY THE FEELING SONNETS

J. H. PRYNNE THE WHITE STONES
Introduction by Peter Gizzi

ALEXANDER VVEDENSKY AN INVITATION FOR ME TO THINK
Translated by Eugene Ostashevsky and Matvei Yankelevich

WANG YIN A SUMMER DAY IN THE COMPANY OF GHOSTS
Translated by Andrea Lingenfelter

ELIZABETH WILLIS ALIVE: NEW AND SELECTED POEMS